misled

susan holbrook

misled

susan holbrook

Red Deer Press

The Publishers
Red Deer Press
56 Avenue & 32 Street Box 5005
Red Deer Alberta Canada T4N 5H5

Credits
Edited for the Press by Nicole Markotíc
Cover design by Boldface Technologies
Text design by Dennis Johnson
Front cover photograph by Graham Law
Printed and bound in Canada by Friesens for Red Deer Press

Acknowledgements
Financial support provided by the Canada Council and the Department of Canadian Heritage.

THE CANADA COUNCIL | LE CONSEIL DES ARTS
FOR THE ARTS | DU CANADA
SINCE 1957 | DEPUIS 1957

Canadian Cataloguing in Publication Data
Holbrook, Susan L. (Susan Leslie), 1967–
Misled
Poems.
ISBN 0–88995–215–9
I. Title.
PS8565.O412M57   1999   C811'.54 C99–910506–X
PR9199.2.H5474M57   1999

contents

for Lori Kennedy

Author's Acknowledgements

Some of these poems have appeared in *Capilano Review, absinthe, West Coast Line, Hot & Bothered: Short Short Fiction of Lesbian Desire* and *Fireweed*.

I would like to acknowledge Nicole Markotíc, long–distance editor and friend extraordinaire. My thanks to the following writers for support, critique and inspiration: Fred Wah, Suzette Mayr, Elizabeth Meese, Sandy Huss, Rob Manery, Andrew Klobucar, Dorothy Trujillo Lusk, Deanna Ferguson, Hank Lazer, Bruce Smith. And as always, Kevin Shortt.

crushing secrets

from the museum of old bones

*Please proceed up the ramps
and down the spiral staircase.*

400 DAYS AGO

i went to the dinosaur
museum and saw
the Human Journey
exhibit, amazed to find
every figure, from
the Cretaceous Insectivore
to Homo Sapiens Sapiens,
female. a guy gawking up:
does this mean Man's going
to turn into chicks?

*The surrounding
sediments tell the story.*

Modern Woman towered over me
blue power suit / eyes, heels
fluffy blonde hairdo, big

These frills briefcase. all i saw
was a composite of fetishes
wished she could have been

served as a means a poet or palaeontologist
of display looked with longing at the bare
feet and animal skin shift
of Neanderthal. i went to look
around at all the bones in that
place. i peered at bones,
bonebeds, the ice age, the age
of reptiles, walked around and

around in my white skin, Jurassic
trundled along with white
Only the color has no tour groups, Triassic
foundation in the fossil record.
everything under glass.

350 DAYS AGO

i told a group of friends about the exhibit
that Modern Man was a woman
that Modern Woman was white
that the models *evolving* toward her
grew progressively paler. an evolution
identify their parents of racism
by the distinctive crest. my friends
nodded or shook their heads, both
meaning the same thing, man
can you believe it, and i stunned, man
can you believe that my tumbling words
and my realization came at the same
moment, only then, and even now
the fact of my delayed recognition fights
its way through the censorship
of memory.

35 DAYS AGO

went back because i couldn't believe
my retrospection, and she was gone.
i wondered at the space, curious about who
objected, how many objections. the last woman
in the line–up was now the smaller model
i recognized from Westerns, the pre–colonial
With each successive step Native American
forward into time, with a Hollywood face. *more
information is available.* did not recognize her from last

year, though i soon realized she had been there
(more ways of forgetting). her nameplate read
Cro-Magnon, so the Barbie was not replaced
just missing. i inquired at the desk, learned she
was in central storage for "re-dress" because
In this mount, Stegosaurus prepares to butt
boys had repeatedly torn at her blouse. *a rival*
in the ribs.

30 DAYS AGO

called back to find out what she was wearing now:
two-piece gray suit, V-neck, correction, in the end
they decided to retire her, not because she was white
because she was too "tactile." she would be replaced
by text.

3 HOURS AGO

at the flea mart i got a TimeLife book, *Early Man,* i'd read
1 000 000 years ago. *Chapter 7: How the Savage Lives On in Man* and 4: *Homo*
Erectus: A True Man at Last and *their females.*
Put a Neanderthal in a business suit and send him to the super-
market and he might pass completely unnoticed.

museum infophone: We don't need a model of the Modern Woman
after all you're the Modern Woman!

she sits in central storage, the metaphor screams, ago, ago, glass eyed,
wig on or off? i have reason to want her released, reason to want her
locked away, reason to hope that some time from now all dolls unlock,
cast *known as Lucy, her remains* limbs and dig, get dirt under nails and
bones, dig for each other and excavate the Human Journey, bury the
glass captions, the pedestals, the long wait in line

peaches

(for Denise)

You get tired of all those plums and peaches in lesbian erotica. Peaches are always popping up in sexy poems and stories, to suggest breasts, cunts, succulence. You try to avoid them, but she's making you fall off the wagon. Peaches are all you think about now—their juice, their sweaty rilled pits, their fuzzy fuzzy faces. Falling off the wagon with all those ripesoft peaches rolling around, bumping fuzzily into each other, cruisin for a bruisin. Peaches and cream everywhere you look, thinking, she's peachy keen. At the farmers market you're offered a free one, bite into it and squirt the farmer in the eye. You buy 2 baskets. In high school your friend's mum is a home economist, she makes 12 peach pies in one afternoon. You eat a piece of each, to be helpful. She asks, which did you like best? They're all GREAT! you shout, double over and throw up on her shoes. Seems like you can never keep peaches to yourself. And now this girl tells you she really hates peaches because one time peach Kool-Aid came out of her nose. Instantly you develop a crush. Instantly peaches are important. Very, because all you know about her is two things: she is a goddess and she doesn't like peaches.

You might say the word *lesbian* with a shudder, like there are cooties crawling up your back porch.

You might say the word *lesbian* like you're reading it out of a science textbook.

You might say *lesbian* dustily, like it all happened in Greece a long time ago.

You might whisper the word *lesbian* because it's naughty.

You might smirk when you say *lesbian* because it's funny. Ha ha funny. You can't help but laugh even if they're your neighbours and they're just mowing the lawn or building a cat door.

Young homos look *lesbian* up in the dictionary after school.

You might say *she's A lesbian,* or *she's lesbian* like it's a religion.

Maybe you find out your daughter is a lesbian and now you pick up the word *lesbian* with tweezers.

You might say *lesbian* like it's a euphemism for itself.

You might say the word *lesbian* like it's beyond reproach. Like the word nun.

Maybe you thought you were straight and suddenly find yourself saying the word *lesbian* like every letter is gravity, like you better wipe that dusty smirk off your face.

You might try to say *lesbian* and find yourself stuttering for the first time in your life.

You might say the word *lesbian* like goodbye.

You might say *lesbian* one day and not the next.

You might say the word *lesbian* like it's a pain in the ass.

You might say the word *lesbian* like you're keeping *dyke* for your friends.

You might drool over the word *lesbian*.

You might say the word *lesbian* like salt–water taffy.

You might wipe *lesbian* off your face.

You might say the word *lesbian* with a shudder and say let's do it again, sweet pea.

crush

(for Cindy)

Crush. That's a tame one. That's a word you can have over for Sunday dinner. A blushing teeny–bopper and a puppy with a leather shoe: Aw, you say, she's got a crush. What about all the hearts that have been garbage compacted, steel-toe ground, 18-wheeler run over, grand piano dropped, record pressed, rockslid into bloody rubble? Crush leavened by repetition, and bottles and bottles of orange pop.

I was ready to be a teeny–bopper long before I hit 11. At 11 you couldn't be a teenager but you could be a bopper, wear bobby socks and bop around and the other boppers would get crushes on you. We didn't wear bobby socks in 1978—I got that from my mother—we wore white slippers with pom–poms that poked out the back of our North Star runners. The pom–poms came in every colour, kelly green to maroon. It was a bad year if you couldn't keep matching socks together. I was ready for bopping because I'd been having crushes for years. I knew all about going together and eye contact with boys and pictures of Leif Garrett pinned to my cousin's bedroom wall. Now in my late twenties I am seized again by the crush, this time for shes. Now Leif Garrett doesn't cut it because eyes aren't everything.

Coming out late throws teen and teeny–bopper homo crushes into retroactive relief. Revelation or speculation. Biology, homology, multiple choice. The cool sweaty bliss of holding hands with Eve behind the strip mall, after we shared a grape Mr. Freeze. We were secret best friends, our real best friends not in the know. Janet with such a startling body I stopped being her friend. Donna and I had a spooky spiritual connection, we took a lot of baths together.

Now Eve, I'm at your house and tell you that last weekend Derek wanted to kiss me and I wanted to kiss him too because he's so cute but I said no French kissing because the tongue is gross. Eve, we will melt chocolate chips on graham crackers and watch *Fantasy Island* and try on cinnamon lip gloss and Love's Baby Soft perfume and I'll wear your pink nightie and we'll whisper in one of your twin beds like always and now you're telling me your brother has a crush on me and I'm so happy because he's 2 years older and Eve I want to crush my lips on yours, crush my tongue into your mouth, lie on you in the twin bed. Eve, who's your favourite Hardy boy, Shaun or Parker, and Eve I want to crush you.

Janet I know your teen body better than the boy I slept with for 2years who gave me a pre-engagement ring. Janet I fixate on your every curve and decide it's jealousy. It must be that I want what my boy's body in my boy's jeans and cupless undershirt doesn't have. Your filled-out underwired seat-splitting shape. I want it. You're beautiful and a weirdo. When I come home at 11 pm on a school night with snow all down the back of my winter coat, my father jumps to conclusions, thinks a man has entered my life. It's just a look, he doesn't say much because it's nature's way after all, what can you do. You and I were making angels. Thin ones and voluptuous ones. You thought I dumped you because you were weird and I'd lose face with the popular kids. You were right.

Now when my father arrives from out of town he can't figure out why my woman friend is always around, driving us wherever we want to go. What an angel, he says.

Janet, we cut through the cornfield on the way back from the late showing of *On Golden Pond*. I lie back in the snow and you appear over me, press your angel's weight on me and we fan our legs and wings for an hour. You crush me until I'm wet through.

Donna, in the March break you and I drink Tab and see who can eat the fewest slices of the lemon loaf your mother brought to Daytona Beach. We're both getting gorgeous and we starve and whisper in the hotel bed our sunburns itching and talk about sex and boyfriends. Even though we starve each other we like each other more than anyone. When boys and men get crushes on us we squeal and hug. Once we do it after we've had a bath, our bodies wet and bare.

You say that was weird and we remain at arm's length the rest of the trip. Donna, lie back in the bath, tell me about him and I'll lean down and lick you thin. Lift you close to the surface so I can get a breath now and then. I'm a fabulous swimmer, eating and breathing at once, starving for all the lemon loaf. You'll start to feel hungry too, and you'll kick and flail under my eating and knock the shampoo to the floor.

A couple of years later you tell me you're a lesbian and not only that but your therapist thinks. You and I. I say *really* and hang up and tell my boyfriend you'll never believe this. Next time I see you I'm afraid you'll kiss me and I can't see your body anymore. You are crushed that I'm so stupid.

In my late twenties the crush enters like a beautiful wrecking ball. I crush everything I know including a man I like more than anyone. Love more than anyone. Everyone is crushed that I'm so stupid.

Eve is a gorgeous restaurant manager in Regina, Janet has a husband on TV, Donna you send me a postcard that says are you ok.

Learning her colours, how to tell time, how to share, read, multiply, square dance, comprehend photosynthesis, these were the official curricula. But she soon discovered the real point of going to school was to study the management of bodily fluids. Learn what stays inside, what can go out. A few tears were ok, snot was not. Intentional spit cool, inadvertent spit grotesque. Blood from your knee was noble, blood from your nose was just red snot. Such fine-tuning would follow the more critical scenes of kindergarten, where the transgressions were extravagant and dripping with portent. She watched tiny Amy Grace stand up for show and tell, blink nervously and peeeeeeeeeee and knew that that kid was transforming, with every passing piddling second, into someone against whom the others would define themselves. During storytime one afternoon, right in the middle of the cross-legged gaggle, a little boy threw up his lunch. Kids shrieked and scattered but she didn't budge because there, undigested, floated all the macaroni letters of the alphabet. They had been singing their ABCs not 10 minutes earlier, and this rendered the puke uncannily relevant. It was at that moment, seeing the alphabet scrambled all out of order, that she realized her favourite letter, Elemeno, was not one.

Approaching puberty, she met the immanent texts of grade six, the scandalous books of Judy Blume. Judy Blume milked the purchase of secrets and secretions that would grease the path to adulthood. Her fluids were of a new ilk: inappropriate in public, but divine in private. Her big-font novels were never in the library, and private copies were passed around like currency. Pride seeped through mock shame when any girl whispered that she had to go to the nurse to get some 'feminine hygiene.' The girls performed horror as Amy Grace's bloody pad tumbled out of her pyjama pants at a sleepover. How unhygienic. Actually, what fell out of her pants this time really was gold.

For girls Judy Blume wrote *Are you there, God? It's me, Margaret*, it was all about periods. For boys there was *Then again, maybe I won't* and the important secretion in this book was Tony's wet dream. But boys didn't read about Tony, girls did. She did. The wet dream was mysterious and shameful and spectacular, reason to cringe when John Lennon sang "I've Got a Feeling" and her parents were in the kitchen with her. *Everybody had a good year, everybody let their hair down* . . . It was coming. *Everybody pulled their socks up.* She and her parents and *Everybody had a wet dream* and all that explosive desire spurting out of the radio, dripping off the light fixture and spangling her father's glasses.

The next year in Life Skills the teacher wrote the secretions on the board, although the girls already knew about them from Judy Blume. She heard again about her bleeding and boys' nocturnal emissions and began to have the peculiar feeling that while the boys were surging and urging, she and her friends were being moulded into wary little Marys. Apparently, Lennon's *Everybody* didn't include her. The teacher never connected the wet dream to her own countless wakings, a pleasurable pulse between clenched thighs, a slippery patch on her nightie. There was no term for girl wet dreams, no word for her sexual secretions. This wasn't like Elemeno, she was sure of this one, and she was onto that teacher, onto those Beatles. She was onto that Tony. She was going to write her own book. Call it *Hey Tony, My Dreams are Wetter than Yours.*

as thirsty as

Only you could carve a pumpkin and make it look aloof. Neck up, it doesn't suck. The more she began to love her, the more she avoided that word. Signed her letters 'Yours', and she was. Embouchure blown out of proportion. Whet with an 'h' is wetter. If language really were transparent, I would like the bathing suits. Always horning in on his own thoughts. As we dance, as wet as. Call your dog 'Toot' or 'Chutney' and it won't grow any bigger. Consider the whistle blown.

Dreams about being starkers for the duration of an anthem. If the figurative does precede the literal, what about falling in love. You got shinier. Men titter too. Tittie is a synonym for sister. As in I spent all afternoon talking with mine. Pell-Mell and Willy-Nilly. Sutured elf. Had the flu, but I'm welling up. Shelve sifting. *Are you happy*, she asks her cat. As light as. As soft as. *Whatever*, grumbled into vittles. Meow Mix the heteroglossia of cats. Later, on the doorstep, the pants end of a mouse.

Makes you sick. You can't wash it out of your mitts. Would you swim through it for money. I'd like to be a gumshoe so I could put my foot in my mouth. Ruthy salutes you. Gather up your bath. To jettison a fine spurt, punctuate sentences that way, hands on worldly hips, or turn away from a conversation of great import just for an instant to frown, spit in the grass. The grizzly tore through the campground, ate the gummy bears out of her pack. Mental note: the green ones are tastiest. As light as. As lime as. An environment where two L's can stand together: *maillot* like *espadrilles* is a word in a novella. Minimalism makes him lonely.

No running no jumping no horseplay. Blue tunes slow the flutter. Stuck with a dumb waiter and a lazy susan. Say 'pips' and sweat peals. When you think of a horseshoe is it on a horse. The music started and balls rolled in sockets. Silk clips. A small seizure of the heart at the thought of buds and pips. As sweet as. Written on the back, sassafras is best. She told me about her lover's single ball and years later I recognized him in the street, couldn't remember his name but knew he had one nut. I said hi. Gone retinal for a name with no middle. Roll–call caesura. Horses must stay in the shallow end. I'd measure this girl in hands.

Too loose too blue too concrete. The mop was floored. Bulbs in the throat. The day you're fat I'll eat my pork-pie hat. Somebody's cranky. You turn mine. Add water to possible squash for a consonant on the side of a plate. Engorged orange. Bleeders yadda yadda yadda. Fur tool. Forsake sauce. Their legs a nest. As orange as, as soft as. Mice find their own children cuter. A cool run down to the ash pile. Budding fire. Loop de loop ennui. Look at the soles of your feet in the mirror. They've been with you as long as your face. As long as, as pink as.

She gave her lip. An itch with no intention. Claw clippings, chips in the aspirin. Cotton batting a soft strike. Now lie in it. A stupor of pedants. Did they ever occur to you. Rounding off makes an 8 and it figures with cream. More laps, fewer dogs for them. Set your watch ahead and she won't drift farther. You'll need some gumption. Bereft of this and that, spend a third of your allowance on the rest of your life. The valentine said I'm nuts about you with a squirrel. A colour for the state of mind in which you floss. Doze through the athletic monitor.

/

Those who thank the bus driver and those who don't. Those who place mugs right side up in the cupboard and those who turn them upside down. Team players and lake swimmers. You believe it's all relative or you don't. Mutual funds. Or not. You drink beyond the point of pleasure or you never get there. Who gets more dust in their cups.

Indecision makes you heroic down the cracks. Don't cut the pink string connecting your mittens. Skate to fall. A tiny sequinned skirt compounding the humiliation. As bright as. As brave as. Her hands fell to the floor at the slightest. Provocation. Moved to memory block. Forget the cortex chock-full of flak. There are birds between names and parts of the brain. Bark sequestering walnut meat. The erotics of such and such meet the poetics of this and that. Thirst. Just be glad it's not a glue storm. That he didn't suffer. That these shoes should last. That you lost a redundant organ. You won't get letters if you don't send them.

Bikinis see scar trouble. Trunks purview. Fresh fruit inseparable. The proper mode of proceeding based on intention, not desire. Tutti patouti. We are asked, when our desires are discovered, what are your intentions. As tutti as. Rapture's contour suits a lush misperception. Lace up hips. A wrap-around controversy. With crown taken, what's the synecdoche for you. The amorous head, the heart of repetition.

*misling the
laureate*

misling the laureate

(for Kevin)

there was a word i used to know fully, it was full-blown, appearing
with the ease and frequency of memos and inappropriate thoughts.
the word i knew was 'misled' [mī' zəld] and it came up all the time in
Trixie Belden, Emily of New Moon, Anne, Nancy, Pat, someone was
always getting 'misled' [mī' zəld]. the infinitive 'to misle' never showed
itself, but i didn't notice, since all the books i read flew in the past.

one day i found out about 'misled' [mis lɛd']. after that, the mysteries
of my heroines became more complex; sometimes they were [mis lɛd'],
and sometimes they were [mī' zəld], an act far more sinister, malice
there, a sour gut. misling, make no mistake, is done with a sneer.

> err or else
> err borne
> bruit Buic
> Bel Air
> leafy plans
> red paint, tin
> scratches divine
> and errant like a knavel
> just popped-out
> i suppose

and 'laurels.' what else could they have been, and what else could they
be, except buttocks, what else but butts. we were supposed to look
down on people who 'rested on their laurels.' the moral Don't rest on
your laurels meaning Don't sit around on your ass. laurels was just a
polite way of saying it, so that laurels meant buttocks in a vague way,

vaguely buttocks in the fashion of vague words like *loins* and *haunch-
es*.

in grade 5 we learned about the victorious Olympian athletes who
had laurels placed on their heads. that was my first pornography.

Charles Bernstein: . . . *I want to suggest that poetics must necessarily involve
error. . . . Error as projection (expression of desire unmediated by rationalized expla-
nation): as slips, slides . . .*

apparently, after Daphne frustrated Apollo's attempts to rape her, the
angered god transformed her into a laurel bush and broke off a
branch. mythical residue of the word: a symbolic rape our wreath of
distinction. there every time i read the word 'laurel.' but i look both
ways, and this will never never edge out the half a plain bum, bony
or freckled, vague, powdered, blue-veined, fire engine cheek that can
sit flat on a chair or go about posturing with celebrity dreams.

slips, slides. slipping when you stay in the pool because your suit's
worn thin or after a bad flip turn it slips to expose a nipple, fish-kiss
(for how long) now the shower tile oddly green-white not pink-white
will it take a naked man to point out the error of your oops why yes
it will stranger alert to your leg blood running down exit down by the
shallow end and on the way home in the snow hair freezes into sticks
boys throw insults, Suck me Off! Suck *me* Off! i shout back, at a loss,
stars recede, breath and snot frozen, hair chiming in the ears.

Things Learned through Trial and Error:
>   DON'T PUT YOUR TONGUE ON THE ICY CHAIN-LINK JUST SO
>   YOU CAN SEE WHAT ALL THE FUSS IS ABOUT.
>   DON'T EAT FIVE TACOS AND THEN RUN FOR THE BUS.
>   DON'T SQUEEZE FROGS.
>   DON'T SMOKE CIGARS.
>   DON'T BE SMUG.

DON'T WEAR PINK AND ORANGE TOGETHER.

many of my mistakes were generated out of a misling logic of hybridity. so when I burst through the front door after swim practice and shouted 'I'm RAVISHED' it was because that was the only word which went hip to hip with 'famished' and 'ravenous.' in these cases mistakes were about words that live next to each other, mistakes only trying to be neighbourly.

> in french dogs say
> oiau oiau
> english dogs take a bow
> a bow, a laurel
> marrow brow
> bone dogs take the prize, laura.

in grade 2 we learned about abbreviations like Dr. and etc. i was all for this economical idea, and started to sign my work Susan Hol. my name as big as Incorporated, anybody could fill in the rest.

Freud says *We notice, too, that children, who, as we know, are in the habit of still treating words as things, tend to expect words that are the same or similar to have the same meaning behind them—which is a source of many mistakes that are laughed at by grown-up people.*

Big Bird posits
big people
small people
matter of fact all people
everyone makes mistakes so why can't you.

there was that other admonition, Don't burn your britches. i got a whiff that this had to do with friendship somehow, and that there was some connection with liar liar pants on fire. the main point was don't play with matches around your britches, the danger being of course that you might ultimately burn your laurels, and then you couldn't rest on them if you wanted to.

most of my mistakes clatter around the body, my contradicting tattoos.

does your tongue recoil at mistaken objects, salt for sugar, butter for cheese, wasabi for toothpaste, potpourri for popcorn, croquettes for coquettes questions for Christians crêpes for craps caps for cups tit for tat that's that nough's enough loose lips slink slips.

Nicole Brossard: *Very young, I perceived language as an obstacle, as a mask, narrow-spirited like a repetitive task of boredom and lies. Only poetic language found mercy in my eyes. . . . Very early I had a relationship to the language of transgression and subversion.*

i was not as precocious. when i was younger i didn't know when i was on the wrong side of the Law. my errors, my subversions, were unconscious, secreted and embraced somehow by my skin, nerves, blood, a body threatened by language which was slowly misling it.

some mistakes are shared. nicole mar. and i admit to each other that we wondered how to eaves trough on a conversation. this is the radio of gossip, accumulated shinglings of omission and desire, rumour pours, humours splash to the dirt and the roof is dry and correct.

error happens all the time in songs. i still believe there is a wee olive in a yellow submarine.

> DON'T LEAVE YOUR CONTACTS IN A GLASS OF WATER BY THE
>   BED AND THEN GO TO SLEEP THIRSTY.
> DON'T BUY A CAR "AS IS."
> DON'T KNOCK A THIRD KNEE, IT COULD COME IN HANDY.

DON'T EAT BLUEBERRIES RIGHT BEFORE AN INTERVIEW. DON'T TELL HAIRDRESSERS TO DO WHATEVER THEY THINK IS BEST.

the other kids in grade 8 told me i had an innocent face. boyfriends complained this made it difficult to French kiss. in library period, Carlo Pica would try to get a laugh, sea-water stare, test my sexual knowledge. hey Susan, do you know what a hard-on is. hey, do you know what masturbation is. hey Susan, do you know what a blow job is. my answer, always a studied don't-waste-my-time *du-uh* to all these questions, was most indignant to that last one, though i refused to elaborate, my image of the act far too gorgeous. they could have their stupid hard-ons and laurels on their heads and so on but the blow job was my spectacular cinema. my image of the first part would have conformed to Carlo's i guess but the climax I imagined was errant: i would raise my head, puff out my cheeks and high C blow a chromo-somal fire-burst all over the wriggling chest of my Olympian victor.

Susan Bordo says our automatic bodies can work against us. the *docile, regulated body practiced at and habituated to the rules of cultural life* can throw our conscious politics out to sea, a salute smacks you in the forehead before you even gave an order to the tiny men in yellow hard hats lounging in your neural pathways. but what if it also works the other way around: what if your crossed-eyes, your gas, your tying tongue are more radical than you are

> what a ghastly
> mistake
> boo boos
> terrify, spine-
> crack
> shingle out
> throatings
> of boudoir

there is mousse
on the roof
of your mouth!
furniture burns

laurels
of the sorrel mare
what a sorry
sorry wheelbarrow
horse
but listen
go this way
faltering takes
time
or that

it wasn't that language misled me. i misled language.

Sidonie Smith: . . . *since woman is necessary for the preservation of the divinely
authored species, scholastics such as Aquinas refused to label her, as Aristotle had, a
monstrous or unnatural creation; instead, they labeled her . . . "misbegotten man."*

that mis– is their take, their pool, their reading lesson. but contradic-
tions well up, clouds of ink or blood obscure and beget.

what is transgressive is the persistence of error, you never learn, i still
misle, acquiring my mistakes at that crucial Piaget time, try to resist
the allure of that Pink Pearl by the hole–punch it will rub your error
into tweedles, consume its own perfect pink martyr self.

DON'T PAY ATTENTION TO YOUR COMPUTER'S SPELL
    CHECKER WHEN IT SUGGESTS YOU CHANGE FEMINIST TO
    FEMME FATALE.
AND DE BEAUVOIR TO THE BEAVER.

DON'T EXCEED DAILY RECOMMENDED.
DON'T KNOW WHETHER 9–1–1 IS REALLY JUST FOR ARROWS
    THROUGH THE HEART OR WHAT.
DON'T GIVE ME LIP, YOUNG LADY.
DON'T LEARN FROM YOUR MISTAKES.

why do I feel
guilty . . .

Why do I feel guilty in the lingerie department at The Bay

After all, I'm a woman, I'm old enough to look casual in here, I'm in my prime, in fact: why not try on a few things, discuss sizes and wires with the clerk like it's nothing, a bit of a chore even, like shopping for sneakers. But I don't feel casual, I flush around all these Vogue Playtex Daisyfresh girlies in their underwear on boxes the size of XXX videos. Today I see you in all the pictures. You're the one smiling off to the left in a flattering ¾ pose, underwired, lace-trimmed, full-figured, in black, white or the lurid 'nude.' I also see you in that emerald green satin bra that's slinking there loose in the bin, boxless. The bin is where the loose women get bras, women like me.

Brah, my mother used to say it, as in *brat*, claiming *bra* as in *draw* was an affectation. Either way is an affectation if you ask me, a way to unpronounce desire, a big cover-up.

I walk over to the bin, my hand goes in. Yes, it's official, I want you in this emerald green satin bra, even though all you ever wear is a white sportsbra. Or sportsbrah. And what if I bought it for you? Maybe you'd go for it. Maybe you'd give up your sportsbra for one evening. Nobody else would have to know. Maybe nothing is more important today than spending $29.99 and easing you into this emerald green satin bra.

"Can I help you?" asks the saleswoman. She's twice my age, pink silk blouse, black sweater vest, lipstick, 34B I think before I can stop myself.

"Yes, I'm looking for socks," I say. But I'm clearly gripping the green bra, my clammy fingerprints all over it. "Do you have this in a C-cup?" I add.

Her eyes dart to my chest, "That's a little large probably, for you."

"Oh, it's not for me it's for my sister-in-law."

My cheek twitches with the lie, so it looks like I'm winking at her.

Her hasty step backward sets a full rack of red lace thongs swinging. I notice she has a nametag that says Erma and a tape measure around her neck, which she now clutches at each end so that it cuts into her flesh like a bra strap that's too tight. There's no way she'll use the tape measure on me. That's for people who are genuinely casual, people with plastic skin and stainless steel nipples, people who would never salivate or lose their breath or get wet under the scuff and tug of Erma's tape measure. My nice woman façade is cracking off in great hunks and Erma can see the dirty old pervert beneath. She looks stunned. Like she's wondering how to protect all those bare-shouldered girls on the bra boxes from my leers, like she's about to call security. Or like she just realized, *oh my god I work in the underwear department.*

Then you saunter in with your baseball cap and your gas station attendant jacket that says Jake and the Sportsmans you just bought in men's wear. You eye the green A-cups in my hand and assume they're for me, lick your lips and break the awkward silence with an *mmm* sound.

Is this your brother? asks a hopeful Erma, clearly more comfortable with incest than dykes. Or maybe she directs your desire toward the absent sister-in-law. That fictional sister-in-law who will make this sale respectable. Poor dear sister-in-law, she's really in need of this bra. Her little Jake says *mmm* and oop—there she goes through the daisyfresh field of Erma's imagination, her breasts flopping around in a family values breeze, crying out for a little satin restraint. *Mmm* I answer, and Erma retreats into the stockroom to get the C. But Brother Jake has got a hold of his sister, refusing to let me take my clammy A-cups back to the loosewoman bin. Looks like we're buying in bulk today. Going for the emerald green satin bra family pak. Maybe later we'll go home and give each other a fitting. Get out the tape measure and play lingerie store. I get to be Erma, and you can be the woman in her prime, getting a little flushed.

Why do I feel guilty in the changeroom at Britannia Pool

After all, I'm a swimmer, I have a Speedo, I can do a flip turn and a shallow dive and I can say "breast stroke" without smirking. I even know that spitting in my goggles will reduce the fog, that baby powder in my cap will stop it sticking to itself. It should be clear to anyone who sees my flipping and diving and spitting and powdering that I am legitimate. That three times a week I mingle with a bunch of naked women and it's all on the up and up. I've been doing it for years, starting at six when I routinely showered at the Y with my mother and her swimming buddies.

I lost sleep over those shower scenes back then, due to the parasite problem. In retrospect I can identify tampon strings as my troubling fixation, but at the time I suffered over how to break it to my mother that she and her friends had worms. Athlete's foot wasn't the only thing you could catch at the pool.

You would think that after twenty-five years, I could feign a little nonchalance. But instead I sneak more peeks, get more flustered when I read that sign "Inappropriate behaviour will not be tolerated in the changerooms," and forget more quarters in the coin-operated lockers as every season brings me closer to my scatty-brained sexual prime. Sometimes, particularly when I'm low on cash, I scan the lockers to see if other girls have left quarters behind. Nobody else has this problem. These are women who gossip in the showers while soaping up their gleaming thighs, then smile calmly into the wild scream of blowdryers, wearing nothing but plush coral pink towels wrapped around their waists, chlorine dripping languorously from suits on hooks. Where did they learn to be so blasé, and why don't they ever forget their quarters?

I learned awhile back not to go to Adult Swim on weekends. I took "Adult" to mean that I could do some lengths in peace, without being blindsided by an inner tube or looking down at my legs later and saying, "Hey, these aren't my Band-Aids." But I found that some guys interpret "Adult" as in "Adult magazines sold here." They lounge in the shallow end. You try to keep your head down as you approach their creepily billowing trunks and the flash of a medallion nestled in chest hair. Beefy arms span the length of the wall and you have to stop short and, in the time it takes you to suck in a breath, one's nabbed you with an irresistible "Lookin' good" or "Can you teach *me* the breast stroke?"

I'm no better. While I usually breathe right, stroke stroke, breathe left, stroke stroke, today I breathe right, stroke, breathe right, stroke, breathe right on the way up the pool, and breathe left, stroke, breathe left, stroke, breathe left all the way back, just so I can keep my foggy goggles fixed on the red suit in the next lane. I'm a creep too.

She's faster than me, she's plump and shiny and slick. She's like the sea lion in the AquaWorld tank, oblivious to me as she undulates past, her nostrils collapsed into slits. I kick as fast as I can, stroke without splashing, imagine I have long wiry whiskers, trying to catch her notice. I want to be in the sea-lion club. When she stops at the end, I stop too and take off my goggles. I spit in them, eager to prove I'm très cool. But instead of hitting the mark clean and sharp, the gob remains slung from my mouth, bobbing like a tiny bungee jumper. She looks over and I forget my lips and smile. Then she's off again like a shot, leaving me and my spittle hanging.

I rest my weary AquaWorld tourist muscles in the sauna. I brought the paper so I don't have to concentrate on where to direct my eyes should any naked women come in. I flip to the personals. The straight section is full of older gentlemen seeking slim ladies and affectionate ladies seeking generous gentlemen. I find the usual chasm between genders in the queer section:

Wimmin to Womyn
GF wants to meet someone who likes music,
laughter, animals and quiet walks. If you're

*looking for someone to share with, let's
make friends and then, who knows?*

Men to Men
*My 8" uncut dick needs a hungry hole to
pump into oblivion. Do you have a bubble
butt and shaved balls? Shoot me a message
and let's see who's more oral.*

Why don't lesbians have a genital aesthetic? Are we too skittish about
objectifying each other? Or could the problem be, as Mr. Rogers
explains, that boys are fancy on the outside, while girls are fancy on
the inside? Is it true that men are just hornier? Do I even know what
kind of pussy I like? Have I ever met one I didn't like? Is it in fact the
lesbians who are so horny we don't have the patience to be discrimi-
nating? I press my back against the hot cedar, close my eyes, and
compose a proper personal:

*My full breasts need some hard sucking
(Ok, they aren't "full," but 8 inches?
Please.) and my long tongue hungers for a
wet snatch with plenty of meat to grab on
to. Can you give up music, laughter, and
animals for a chance to fist me all night,
taking breathers only to receive explosive
comes under my busy lips and fingers?
Would you rather have a quiet walk along
the sea wall or my thumb jammed into
your lubed-up ass as I . . .*

"Hot today, eh?" Sea–lion girl.
"Oh hi. Yeah." I check to make sure my hands still hold the paper.
She isn't wearing her red suit. As she sits across from me with one leg
bent up to her chest and the other swinging off the bench, I note that

her fanciness is not completely on the inside. I swallow and wonder if inappropriate behaviour would be tolerated in the sauna.

"You're a Leo, aren't you?" she says knowingly.

"How did you know?" I gasp, amazed. I'm a Capricorn, but I want to please and besides, her confidence is so dazzling, I've begun to doubt my birthday.

"You have a calm about you, you seem comfortable in your body." Suddenly it's too hot. Why didn't I realize it before, saunas are unbearably hot. Comfortable in my body? Does that mean I look like an old quilt or a one-eyed teddy bear? Are my legs crossed or uncrossed? Do I have worms? I can't remember. I can't breathe. I could pass out. She's still looking at me. The romance novel phrase "her eyes are limpid pools" comes to mind, and now I know what it means. What if I passed out right this minute? I should plan for it, so I can tumble gracefully to the floor without breaking my nose or hip. The tiles down there look nice and cool, a great big ice-cube tray. She's cute. When I come to, I might find her hovering over me, a concerned look on her face, as she fans me with her flipper. I need to run out, take a cold shower, or move down to the lower bench. At least lose this newspaper, which is about to combust in my lap. But I sit still, comfortable in my body.

"Have you had your Saturn's return?" she asks.

"I don't know, I'm . . . I'm from Calgary."

Is 'what's your sign' making a comeback? Did it ever stop working in Vancouver? It's clearly working on me. Why is she so cool? Why don't I put down my paper? I could just put down the paper in a really beyond comfortable way. She's smiling. I'm evaporating. She takes a swig from her Volvic bottle. With a sudden rush of bravado, I toss the paper aside. But with all the heat, it's become affixed to my fingers and I can't shake it. I'm still trying to peel myself off when she gets up to leave. Cool air rushes in as her glossy butt swishes out. The newsprint has made an impression on my sillyputty skin, so now I have "raunchy action" on one thumb and "social drinker" on the other.

I wait a couple of minutes so it doesn't look like I'm following.

47

Slink down to the lower bench with arms extended so I can break my fall if indeed I pass out. Finally I make it to the shower and wash off the sweat, careful also to scrub my thumbs, since she's probably not into labels.

I approach my locker naked, less because of being comfortable in my body than because I don't want her to see that I stole my towel from the Holiday Inn. Her locker's next to mine. She's about to leave, her boots all laced up and she's putting on a black rainslicker. I'm buck naked, but I don't care because I'm a Leo. I put my key in and my quarter pings to the floor. While bending over I glance up, look her straight in the limpid pools, which are discovered dilating and travelling over my skin. She turns pink and bolts for the exit. The door to her empty locker swings open, and I pinch the quarter peeking out of her slot.

Why do I feel guilty at the Canada–U.S. border

After all, I'm a dual citizen. I have a birth certificate from one country and a passport from the other. This duty–free in–between zone should be the one place on earth I am truly at home. But border guards like it simple. "Just tell them you're American," people say. "Save some time." *Lie.*

I've told two big lies in my life and both backfired. The first time I was simmering plastic jacks in apple juice atop my Suzy Homemaker oven when my mother ordered me to tidy my room because it was a "fire trap." I surveyed the mess, heaved a beleaguered sigh, and began to perform the usual short cuts. Dirty and clean clothes balled into a drawer; Battleship pegs, LiteBrite bulbs and candy corn squirreled into the Spirograph box; pipe cleaners, polished rocks, dust balls, Little Golden Books, a tooth, half a carrot all swept into the closet. By the time I returned to my jacks "stew," I was thoroughly bone–weary and decided it would be a good idea to flush it down the toilet. The next day when my mother asked me if I had flushed anything down the toilet I said *No.* This would be a triumphant lie, a sure thing—I'd seen those jacks disappear but good with my own eyes. Easy–bake easy. The plumber came and pulled them up, one by green red yellow one.

The next year I impressed a lot of kids in my class by telling them I'd been on the *Zoom* show. I became a legend, and kids I didn't even know watched for me on reruns. It was a little lie that grew into a sham that became a hoax more difficult to undo with every passing month: "I was only a guest, only one time," I would clarify. More difficult every passing year: "I don't know if they ever even aired the episode," I would shrug. "No, I didn't get to keep the striped shirt, it would have cost me $14.95." The lie–pile building to a steaming heap. In grade 7 kids were still saying, "I heard you were on *Zoom.*" By then I just changed the subject, which seemed modest. Last week I watched a

sitcom where a guy is caught lying on his résumé and finally confess-
es, "I wasn't one of the *Zoom* kids either." My lie will never die. It's
tenacious, infectious. My lie is now prime time.

Which is all to say it's a bad idea for me to lie. Especially to a butch
in uniform. "Got any fruit?" she asks. Fruit, wouldn't want to get into
trouble over fruit, I scan the back seat. "Fig Newtons," I admit, my
stupid squinty face reflected in her sunglasses. Apparently they don't
count.

"What's your citizenship," she asks, without a question mark.

"American?" I answer, with a question mark. I offer her my
California birth certificate.

"Passport," she says.

I hand her my Canadian passport swiftly. Swiftly like a guillotine, a
knife in the back, swiftly like a body without a parachute.

"Pull the car over to the side."

I have an urge to weave and screech, but I putter over to the side
and park like I'm pulling into a parking spot at church. A good citizen
of whichever country she likes best.

I watch in the mirror as she swaggers towards the car, barking into
her walkie-talkie. I feel again the heady free-fall of the *Zoom* days. My
trampoline heart makes finding the door handle a shaky business. Fed
up, she opens my door, keys jangling at her snug-fitting belt.

I'm actually more excited than scared. I guess because I'm being
bad. Because I've never even had a speeding ticket and now I'm in
trouble. Because this might turn out to be a good story, a true story, to
tell my friends later. Because this is no *Zoom* illusion. And most of all
because it's all starting to feel like porn.

She orders me to open the trunk. Shit. I packed all my crap so tight,
there'll be no stuffing it back in. I was saving that jack-in-the-box for
the final stop. She taps the trunk impatiently. I turn the key and it
flies open, jettisons hangers, toilet rolls, and a muffin pan which clink,
bouf, clang to the pavement.

"How can you be patriotic to two countries at once?" she demands.

This is no idle question. She wants an answer and I'm left casting about my brain for some relevant philosophical thread. Do I have *true patriot love?* Patriotism just makes me think of guns and songs and Gertrude Stein driving an ambulance in France. "Would you play on two different ball teams?" she continues, pregnantly rhetorical. Would I play on any ball team? I wonder. Surely I could sing at least one anthem on command. *Oh say Canada! joyeux de nos heureux, land of the free, home of the beaver.* Inspiration springs from a more reliable organ.

"Funny," I purr, reaching up and pulling off her glasses, "I thought we were on the same team."

This moment is so cocky, this double entendre so delicious, no one will ever believe I thought it up on the spot rather than two hours later. I'm acting out a B-movie set-piece: the bad girl pulled over. Gonna use my wiles to weasel out of trouble. Since femmes are often misread as straight, sometimes we have to act spectacularly queer in order to clue in those butches.

Unfortunately, clueless butches are often misread as queer. My border guard snatches her glasses back with an agility most astonishing considering the weight of that rock on her wedding finger. Her other hand grips a little velvet box that surfaced in the explosion. With the X-ray vision induced by my anxiety I picture the familiar assemblage of old earrings, half a joint, paper clips, safety pins, buttons. Buttons-safetypinspaperclipshalfaJOINT. I blanche.

Luckily, I repel her. Now she doesn't want to know what I keep in my velvet box. She tosses it back in, tells me to gather my stuff and have a safe journey.

With one nervous eye on the rear-view, I drive away attempting to divine the moral that one expects will cap off a story about lying. A number of lessons emerge as surely as jacks out of a toilet: 1. Don't flirt with the Law if you want to get south of it 2. Objects in the mirror are straighter than they appear 3. You can take any fruit over the border as long as it's hidden in a cookie.

Grim

Then she was forced to put on the red-hot shoes, and dance until she dropped down dead.*

ORTISSIMO ROMANCE, blistered to the max. Rather be ghoulish than girlish, or take salts and calm the fever, sitz baths drown out the whinnying. The subject of pathos or bathos or Cheerios. The Spanish soap opera interrupted by an ad for *peenay sol* and a tree burst through the roof. Stole the show. Narrative is all fun and games until someone loses a roof. Come–uppance is no coin, a warning no prism. And does taking too long to smooth the chenille fall between the cracks of lust and sloth. It's not in grace but in a burning house that we say there is a god. The creepy guy sold me cinnamon gum, saying *so you like Big Red.*

*Italicized lines are gratefully stolen from *The Complete Grimm's Fairy Tales* (New York: Pantheon Books, 1944).

54

He cried: "It was not I, it was my brother," but say what he would, they cut off his head.

MEANWHILE BROTHERS DRINKING LATTES. Meanwhile the axe dulls and thoughts hang by a thread. Froth to blame, blood to fathering wuthering. All manner of amnesias trying to recognize my own neck from that angle. Proving fables can be cerebral. Take heed, he started it but I got in heck. A flustered justice, fresh ground hot flash. Necklace of coffee beads in the bottom of a wax cup. Licking chops. Eyes, beads, lust collecting dust. See what he would, chopping sucks. The evil brother always remembers to send a card on mother's day. "Not I," said the little red hand.

And the ungrateful son was forced to feed the toad every day, or else it fed itself on his face; and he went about the world knowing no rest.

TOAD ON THE FACE BEATS a chip on the shoulder, a poker up the butt. A tinkle in the eye. Sometimes it did. The toad finds you unsightly, clings to your scarred face as to the notion of a transformative kiss. The artist formerly knowing no rest. Ingrates do get familiars, a little chit-chat through sleepless nights. A little ribbing before the hunger. Horns for peace blown in vain. Parents have grateful sons and a mortgage to worry about. Clammy hams, remember hymns, croak out a few. Foraging to save face, just want to be a bump on a log for once. Bilingual duets interrupted by the daily assignment. A grudging love does blossom.

Immediately the physician fell on the ground, and now he himself was in the hands of Death.

THEM REQUISITIONED APPLES. Fell before he got a chance to find a lover worthy of the plums in the icebox note. A moan bigger than a bruise. Bus drivers make the worst passengers. "Cold hands, warm heart," said Death. Good times, bad liver. Grapes in the crisper do not adequate his teeth among stones. Eye them roll, tiny decapitations. Finally a moment to acknowledge the glassiness of the word *tincture*. Praying for a referral. Someone with teeth to say: without, incurring dreams. Within his bending sickles compasse come sorry chips and leaks.

One of them noticed a gold ring on the little finger of the murdered girl and, as it would not come off at once, he took an axe and cut her finger off. But it sprang into the air, over the cask, and fell straight into the bride's bosom.

P AYING FOR PACKAGING. The meanings of cleaving, the digital sound of collateral booty. Is this a lesbian episode. Violence the big tip-off. The admission of certain "feelings" stalling the ceremony. If bosom is singular, how could it fall in, how conceal a scissors. You may now give her the finger. Dotted trajectories score freeze-framed villains, floor X'd with duct tape. Released due to the improbability of the facts. Disbelief, clemency, bugs in a rug. More than duende, jock itch and jiggers spur haunting. This doesn't feel like popcorn. Her finger the memento mori of functional value. How often is duct tape used for ducts.

And behold it was a great castle, and everything inside was of silver and gold. She married him, and he was rich, so rich he had enough for all his life. Let no one ever say that any-one who is silly cannot become a person of importance.

WHOEVER SAID THAT. President's Choice pantyhose toast Gumpy philosophies. He, in a higher register, prefers control top. In monopoly, boys were meant to choose the top hat or cannon, girls the iron or thimble. To 'go slumming' presupposes exteriority. She didn't care about the dough, she liked him for his mesh head. I chose the dog. You be a silver scooper. Gold poised over wish lists, simultaneity, taboo, seeds for weather. Who financed your new lease on life. Yapped at the heels of what tender. I couldn't really stay in the red plastic hotel, but I could use the thimble in a pinch.

Then said he: "Wife, now that you are Pope, be satisfied, you cannot become anything greater." "I will consider about that," said she.

THE OFFHAND COMMENT that chipmunks don't make good leaders. And a couple right there in the yard. Nerve, cheek, balls, gall. Carving. Under that hat you'll find a nut. In that nut ambition rattles. In the rattle a flake of pepper traversed by a mite dreaming of becoming the pope. An indefinite article precedes the rest of us. Best of all, consider about ring kisses. King-sized seats. Quotes open and close around your every poop. Said the satisfied, said the become. Crave bothered touch. Hot doves loitering about her toilette. Implored he, "Forget thunder, douche." Flap and lathered.

And when the poor beast hopped on its three legs, they could only think that it was picking up a stone to throw at them.

KNOCK THE PINS RIGHT OUT from between defensive driving and road rage. Rocks sharper than your phobia of what I'm missing. One hand clapping sounds like the other in a holster. Air suspect over sloping shoulders. Faery snipe. The chocolate bunny misses an eye. Needless to say we panicked and tore away from Easter. Sip soap. I'm a loper, I'm a groper, I'm a midnight Timbit. You brought out the best part of me and threw it. As long as the horse isn't hurt. Stunt mutt. Candy lenses stashed above the K–mart stock girl's retainer. The optic nerve! Does her minimum wage get your hackles. She cackles, a blue and yellow crab drops.

The wild boar, however, had not been able to hide himself altogether; one of his ears was sticking out.

ELF-CONSCIOUS? Why not tape your knees to your head each night. Smut in arrears. Either snoop or root. Be kind, my feelers are out. And hardly had the parking lot attendant handed them a ticket, before his glass house filled with peacock feathers. Wax ball in the jaw a dead wishing, place face down on the dish. Profligate eggs. I know you're in there, the apple of your eye just rolled out. Toll a feathered metre. My tusks are made of handlebars, my motorcycle jacket of fruit leather. Ain't no flies on hardly. Do my beans show, do my fathers, do my druthers.

The bean thanked him most prettily, and as the tailor used black thread, all beans since then have a black seam.

B Y A HAIR, SAVED FROM SPILLING. Thanking most threadily for small white confidences. Hyphen chili. I really did count them for a living. For the soy dust, hard to wink, where in the world have you prettily been. Stitched her up, bellies since then lovingly. A hyperactive brat on a good day is "full of beans." Down the back of your leg, pencil in absent fashion. Have you ever seen her bean green over blue. Beautiful Nauseant. Pork and wieners. On that same good day, larvae wriggling in seeds are "Mexican jumping beans." Kiss my seams when I fall apart at them.

"Yes," answered the cat, "you will enjoy it as much as you would enjoy sticking that dainty tongue of yours out the window."

I T'S THE HOUSE WITH THE PINK WIMPLING. Wet bell. A big French kiss for Summer, blow November. Out the gopher hole of experience comes the furtive muster. Packing lustre, lick trust. Assuming all her life that sticking her tongue out was an invitation, by now her dainty heart hung about her heels. Dragging scowls. Knowing another's enjoy. Another joy, another jolly. Shutters akimbo. Creaking thighs anticipate dollar days, an address to the street, the casement itself answering yes.

The lion in his great haste put his master's head on the wrong way round, but the huntsman did not observe it because of his melancholy thoughts about the King's daughter.

MOCKED THE ASS-BACKWARDS until he realized it was his own. Rubberneck, knee-jerk, tummy tuck, lunch a bust. The King's daughter would put it all behind her. Tragic acorn, that I might be nobody's wife. It's easy to hoodwink the melancholic. Are there no soft C's in this defensive posture. A desert bleached ribcage to cushion the worm coming up next. They told me boiled okra is "interesting, like snot." Tissue in the lion's paw hold still blow out the chairback before she sees nicely nicely done sir.

"I can strangle wolves and bears, but I cannot protect myself from these earth-worms."

THE PROBLEM WITH LOCATING THE NECK. Or it's all neck, from stem to stern. Your body a can of them. Worm a verb, as duck or weasel. Whereupon she named her new pasta sauce, "Bravado!" Water-fish air–bird computer–geek deckle edged. Easel out of the clean and jerk, and too soft for constellations. I can drive the big rigs, but no uni-cycle. Draw me trying, translucent pinkies underwheel. To aerate, like the wolf her moon, the bear her cupboard, the hen her wishes.

After a while, a second giant took the drummer, and stuck him in his button-hole.

TENDER LITTLE DRUMMER. High–hat meringue. The sparing a close call: had the giant preferred hooks. Had the giant already a boutonnière. What would gender do. Bouffant, slouch, the east side of the shirt. Pacemaker. Want darling?—the drummer's own buttonholes. Kitten paper. A giant's head always North. Does bigness or smallness make a hand paw–like. In other words, for whom will you cry if the rescue fails.

out-takes from
rewriting

out-takes from rewriting

A close scrape with death always makes us want to rethink our lives or, to be more candid, rewrite it wherever possible.

−Sky Lee

Last week in the lobby at my grandma's condo I passed a framed meditation. Maybe it was the pastel embroidery thread or maybe I exceeded the condo speed limit, but I didn't get a chance to read the whole thing. All I remember is: *Memories are like pockets.* . . . I suppose I was being cocky by not stopping to read the punchline, suppose I thought it would follow me out the door like the accent aiguë of a cliché. Instead I drove out of the parking lot without a clue as to how memories are like pockets. On the plane home I tried to satisfy the equation. *Memories are like pockets . . . you really only need two.* Or maybe *Memories are like pockets . . . sometimes you find gum. Memories are like pockets . . . they're always on your ass.*

Is it really my story if the memory begins from the driver's point of view? I look through the windshield at the back of a small girl walking at the edge of the gutter. Blonde hair to the waist, pink shorts, red and white T-shirt that says Canada '72, though I haven't seen the front of it yet. I know I was wearing that; it became a crucial element later as I struggled to establish his m.o. The T-shirt was the only motive I. Can't remember what shoes I was wearing because he never saw them.

The third time I wrote this I had an ear infection. My head was flopped over to one side so the drops would sink in. Everything I wrote looked vertical and sad like a concrete poem.
Rewriting is an act of self–love.

Maybe I should rewrite this as a romance.

> Growing an ovarian tumour during the months leading up to an explosive discovery of dyke desire is too fitting a dramatization of hypotheses linking repressed sexuality with cancer. The body saying, unequivocally, 'I will not be gainsaid.' That it is a gynaecological tumour coinciding with lesbian sexuality is just too classically hysterical, too pleasing in its reverberations, in the manner of an anthologized short story or a smug psychoanalytic case study.

Rewriting is self–translation.

translation: to convey to heaven without death. to enrapture.

in the gap between your front teeth, between slibido and libidos, whistling gains ground breezy displacement la rue for you

I shall not throw my eraser across the classroom.
        Ice allot through mire sure crows thoughtless um.
        Eyes aloof wires scarecrows toothless one.

Playing telephone is a kind of translation. It's not that you got it wrong; you heard what you wanted to hear. There were those of us who screwed up on purpose. Knowing that no one could ever prove I was the transgressor, I did it compulsively, just like at the skating rink when the girl with a new cherry chapstick would say *Don't anybody eat it!* before passing it around, I could never resist sinking my teeth into the wax just a little. Lips against the pink whorl of another girl's ear I would tell her lies. Cherry or minty deviance breathed into the small hole, drum roll, tantalized by her innocence of my maverick intentions, tantalized by the possibility that she, too, might whisper on the wild side.

The gutter: deep, hot, swampy. Leaves cling to each other, rot. The hairy hearts of mangoes float. Leaves huge, as if cut from a flag. Leaves at the rim stick to my shoes. I remember now: white sandals, buckles rusting. The shorts are not pink, are thin stripes of red and white. I swerve towards the edge and brake, trapping her. She pretends to search the gutter for something. Can this be the real story if I remember it in English? "Hey, hey, come here, come look in the car."

The students study a lot of lesbian erotic poetry in class. They read about sea life and vanilla wafers, and it's all so hot she doesn't notice her stomach busting out of her pants. By the time she figures it out it's so big they run out of fruits to compare it to. The doctor in emergency tells her she's hyperventilating, his own mouth-hole too small for his face. His cheeks bellow behind the taut ring of his lips, set only to pronounce

something like mon dieu mon dieu, he tells her,
"Your tummy certainly is out of proportion with
the rest of your habitus." Consoles her by telling
her about a woman whose tumour had to be
taken out with a chain lift. "You won't need a
chain lift," he laughs, inadvertently whistling.

swimmingly refute
redundancies
coming back up on
Suzette's corned beef

a wraparound controversy
skirts paranoid snapshots
polar crossings
transheroic dogs

Habitus kicks
Rooster Sleepover Short–lived
and over your head
rapture's Basket

Things you can rewrite:

things you've said that made someone say, just listen to yourself
things you've said that hovered in the air like a fart
things you've said that stuck to the ceiling like your best friend's
    Sylvester the cat helium balloon that you grabbed, tore out of the
    house with, and released in the backyard, just to see if
she didn't invite you to her next birthday party
you can rewrite that too
things you didn't say to the person who said just listen to yourself

things you didn't say to the person who said o don't worry I'm not a
    feminist or anything
you can rewrite cruel things other people say, and turn them into
    compliments
like "you're such a loser" into "you're a really good sport"
you can rewrite a character that is just a bit too family
you can rewrite a family history
rewrite the recipe for lemon–butter sauce, 3 times over, because the
    garlic keeps turning blue
the diary you burned, whether you like it or not. the moment it was
    gone, it began rewriting itself in your head
names on trophies
photographs in yearbooks
you can rewrite the bus schedule, but you might just confuse yourself

> The tumour is a gift. She walks around in a daze, shocking herself, shocked at losing her marriage, shocked she can't stop hurting people she loves, and here is the gift of punishment. Obsessed with cunnilingus she gets cards from in-laws saying god bless you mon dieu god bless you and coming out of the anaesthetic she sees Jesus spelled backwards is sausage.

Maybe I could rewrite this into an embroidered wall hanging.

Maybe it was *Friends are like pockets. Friends are like pockets . . . sometimes they have money you forgot about.*

Friends are like pockets . . . when you're nervous you can put your hands inside them.

15 years later, in Barcelona, my accent was so good they thought I was stupid, not foreign. In a heated discussion with the landlady over our alleged daily shower-taking, I actually said, in Spanish, "I can't tell you how much it hurts me that you call my husband a liar," something I would never say in English. Rewriting this now, it occurs to me that this is probably less due to a purportedly inherent emotionalism in the Romance languages than to the fact that I learned Spanish in Caracas, at the age of 7, by watching the night-time soap opera, *Mariana de la Noche*.

Maybe I could translate this into a rule-book.

How to play Hopscotch:

1. *Place your stone in the first square of the figure.*

Could never figure out what scotch had to do with it.

2. *Hop over your stone and through the unoccupied squares to the end of the figure.*

My grandparents drank scotch, and I couldn't imagine them playing very well, especially late on a Saturday afternoon, when the roast was taking its time.

3. *Jump and spin 180°. Hop to the starting point, pick up your stone on the return.*

Then I found out my dad made beer with hops, and I concluded this was a drunkard's game.

4. *With each turn advance your stone one square.*

Maybe a sobriety test like walking the straight line for a policeman, only this was harder because you were on one leg.

5. *Only step within the unoccupied squares of the figure.*

Now I see in the O.E.D. that a scotch is "an incised line or scratch," that we were hopping the scotch, fervently leaping the line all recess long

They have to tell her 5 times, because she is so doped, that her tumour is benign. She considers sending out cards: *It's Benign!* it would say on the front, and inside she would report its healthy weight and give it a currently popular name like Brittany. What does a benign tumour look like? Was that jagged chafing at her liver and bladder a gaggle of balloons or a mess of proliferating happy faces? Ten days later the official patholo–gy report comes back. 'Interestingly,' says her surgeon, 'we did find some cancer after all.' 'How interesting,' she says. The card would now have to say, *It's a mucinous tumour showing focal areas of tufting with stratification, mild cribriforming, mitotic activity and cytologic atypia!* so she scraps the idea. Now she has a 'Medical' file in her filing cabinet— it comes right before 'Men in Feminism.'

The second time I wrote this my pupils were still dilated from my appointment with the eye doctor. I looked very sympathetic. It made all the difference.

After the girl approaches the car and looks in the open window, squinting, I lose sight of her. That's when an untranslatable desire becomes part of the story. Fly gapes, fingers promote his dick. The expectation of some reaction to it. Looks sad, a day-old balloon animal. "Stay there, come on, how do you like this?" Three rifles lie on the seat beside him. He fumbles for them, tries to hide them under his leg. They clank together like toppling bowling pins. His eyelids keep dropping. "Now, stand in the road, in front of the car, go on, please, just stand in the road, no problem." He's smiling, but I can see his desperation for this favour. The fender nudging my right leg, and to my left the gutter, flanked by a cinderblock wall.

that 'now' of the
marginal, guttural
uttered run-off
coursing at the mouth
offers.

that scrawl in
the gutter, a caress
buss the sticky
thesaurus at
a loss for words.

that parenthetical
parent ethical in
the wings
under yours
transit.

into the gutter muck   sludge   running
        the slowed effort   of nightmares   where
rising snow pulls legs down   where voice is
blown back into your throat   splash and
stuck   clutch at mortar   dragging feet
mud–packed blocks   moving as fast as   as
fast as   the car puttering alongside on impulse
roars away around the block   around and
back   but not before i've made it   to a
busy street   where it merges   any car
into cars

The first time I wrote this I was feverish, thought it was really something, had a thermometer undertongue. your lips (did you know?) are an extension of the red inside of your mouth. Some people write second third fourth fifth seventeenth draughts. There is never a text, just a last draught. Some people are draught–dodgers, say It's draughty in here, close the window.

When I finally arrived, breathless, at Mrs. Hardy's, I couldn't tell her I was no longer sweet. So I just told her about the three rifles that a man pushed under his leg that clanked like bowling pins, and told her the wild story about the man cutting me off and wanting to kill me.

She saw my blush and stutter and didn't know
the lie was not in what I said but in what I with–
held. She told me to go out back and hose off
my shoes. The actress who plays both the evil
twin, Marta, and the angelic twin, Mariana, used
to live in Mrs. Hardy's house.

flawless formance
per loud cousin's
fiancé drumroll

haunting dition
ren to town
buyer crush

sweet prano
so why gender
cut throat

resonant ass
b flat tire
doctor conductor

The last time I wrote this my tumours, lovers, losses had thrown me for
some big loops and the idea of a man showing me his meat and veg
when I was 7 seemed like small potatoes.

The translator finds 'soft against the shins' in 'douce sur les mollets.'
Mollets meaning 'calves,' not shins, this was a clear case of twisting a leg
around just for the sound of it.

Her transformation begins with one birthday
kiss. A kiss which confirms the warnings of her
grade 7 life skills teacher, who had no use for her
since she was flat-chested and no good at gym-
nastics, and who counselled with a trembling
voice: Don't kiss, because kissing will lead to
necking. Don't neck, because necking will lead to
petting. Don't pet, because petting will lead to
heavy petting. Don't heavy pet, because that will
lead to the three kinds of sex: 1. vaginal 2. oral 3.
anal.

see sportscar wishes
taken a toll i am maillot

lining under
shallow utopia
taken a pool for a rough loop

speedos clairvoyant
kick-ass
sound wobbly elbows

She gets the third kind of sex from a resident at
the cancer clinic. Every two months after her
surgery, they give her an internal exam. First the
vaginal exam, about which the male doctors
seem oddly apologetic and anxious. It's not that
terrible—a gloved finger, a nurse's hand to
squeeze—but they always seem flustered, as if
she'll feel deflowered or something. The anal
exam hurts. A lot. But they relax, then, as if it's

an afterthought. She glares at the pink poster of a womby cross-section and noting her grimace, they always try to distract her. "So, what kind of poems do you like to write?"

In the movies writers are wasteful. They type one sentence, maybe a couple of words, rip out the page, crumple it, toss it into a basket full of other crumpled papers. New sheet. Type the same two words. This is not rewriting, this is ritual. Garbage is never so clean. The audience sweats in the dark, tossing crumpled popcorn into their mouths, jumping to conclusions.*

The seventh time I wrote this it was all in the first person. The next time I write this it will end up that way again.

*notes for revision:
1. take out the part about the anal exam. too embarrassing.
2. find out why memories are like pockets
3. take out silly parts
4. and too serious parts
5. take out the notes for revision when you're finished.

tuscaloosa news

Neighbor Helping Neighbor
As Going Gets Tough, First Lady Rises to Top
The Health Gap Between Blacks, Whites Persists
Are *Smaller* Schools *Better* Schools?
Teacher Suspended for Distributing Bibles
House Impeaches Clinton / Balloon Team Sails Over
    Mediterranean

       * * *

just as pine
nut may become
one word

dunno little ticky-
tacky arrow

       * * *

what's pop

becoming difficult
to resist coincident local
windbreaks of Jesus
/football

What Would the First
Lady Do?

       * * *

in the thin

pie piece or
short bar
you see money
is health, heal
th money im
balance due
to the persistence
of statistics

* * *

are *bigger*
friends *better*
friends louder
frogs lower
mortgages friendlier
bets stinkier
sparks shrewder
heartaches colder
tea cloudier
silencer *Napier*
necks

* * *

they call
garters suspenders
we called
suspension
a holiday, a cat
kneading her sweater
in the South is "making
biscuits," a bauble
in every hotel room

* * *

House Impeaches
Clinton Balloon
Team Sails Over
Mediterranean

proleptic

1

To divine the signature superstition.

The point across a pained expression.

Aghast, flabber.

If the rind gives over ogled easy.

Kipper guessing.

Coral shouts.

The idea to perforate the moment you're in.

The owners of Gemland skipped town after dumping
a truckload of costume jewellery into the lake.

Choral oats.

I read prediction in your surprise.

At your own risk.

R's rolled.

Bit by bit slipped out of mind.

Unravelling the beach.

Let me say, in advance.

2

And fortunate. Pork futures.

A wet bath mat as good as an invitation.

To the cat to pee on it.

I before E. The principal is your "pal." Remember the "br" in February, the peach in impeachment, the you in masturbation.

Leave a long-winded message.

That deer's a dead man.

Big plastic roseate.

The taxi in parataxis.

3

What the bride wore.

Set a trap.

Demonstrates a stunning lack of depth.

He had been trying for a far-reaching stupidity.

On any wet bath mat.

Green glass facets pinched and put.

It's the kind of affair to which I wear a hat.

To what do the quotation marks refer in "Absolutely" No
   Parking.

"To which To what" will fool any redbreast into mating.

4

Late slips.

Wanting the jewels in every sentence.

Photos.

Sapphires.

A saxophone choir.

The tail feathers of the bride were covered in bows.

The card reader says ask me anything I say am I a queer she
says I can't answer a question like *that* then flips over the
cards and says what do you know. You are.

Book of correlations.

Queen of diamonds.

Dragonfly suit.

The bathtub copy inspiring, swollen.

5

Seventeen minutes.

Thrown rice pricked at their squinting faces.

"Please" insert deposit slip.

In Canadian time that's twenty-four minutes.

Garnet spoons an idea.

Let's hurt the deer just a little, so it knows to be afraid
of humans.

Gorgeous juicy garnets in my lunch.

This may hurt.

Like laughing hurts.

6

Darling, you're so gemmy.

Two cats with two eyes might mean two one-eyed cats.

How imprecise our contracts.

Immunize yourself with emeralds.

Get to the tailfeathers of the situation.

The book says we'll know the sparrow because he says *poor
Sam Peabody, Peabody, Peabody.*

All told, there were marching mice, happily ever, forwarding.

Even though it was now called "venison" I did not want to eat it.

Forgive and get aquamarine.

Thrown from a boat.

7

You will know my mother because she says *for Petey's sakes,*
    for Petey's sakes.

Birthstones are counting.

Semi-red.

Butcher's juice.

Lake bottom encrusted with credits.

Am I at least semi-precious to you.

Say photograph and we'll take your cheese.

Inside jokes of snow.

He said hurry up hurry up we're going to miss the train even
    though he meant we were going to try to catch it.

Family erected her closet in a day.

Grimacing barn-raisers, schedules smear.

The sun came out and the snowman's face fell.

Swimmy day.

Flippant.

8

Spines agree, wear flippers.

Two eyes made out.

The comet is down for the count.

Your bracelet without a wrist.

Have a gold tooth, and people will say what a character.

Long in the arrangements.

It's more romantic to miss the train than to catch it.

Greater ironies would follow.

Opals not thin.

When he died she had her own name carved in the marble,
    along with her birth date and a dash.

Waiting for the next train anticlimactic.

Reference points sparkle.

PHOTOGRAPH BY LORI KENNEDY

SUSAN HOLBROOK is a poet and fiction writer whose work has appeared in numerous magazines including *Open Letter, Gay and Lesbian Literature, absinthe magazine, hole magazine, West Coast Line,* and *Capilano Review* and in the anthologies *Hot & Bothered: Short Short Fiction of Lesbian Desires* and *Beyond the Orchard: Essays on bpNichol.* She has done graduate work in English Literature and has taught as an elementary teacher in Abu Dhabi. She has worked as an editor, research assistant, swimming instructor and university professor. Susan Holbrook is currently at the University of Alabama completing research on a book about Gertrude Stein.